Developing The Entrepreneur Mindset Of Your Child

By: Daniel Colson

Copyright 2019 All rights reserved.

Developing The Entrepreneur Mindset in Your Child is dedicated to my son. I am so proud of you and how far you have come. I am enjoying this journey with you I am so excited about your future! You are such a great little businessman.

-Fill their life and their bedroom with assets, not liabilities.

Contents

Description 3
Introduction: The Entrepreneur and Mindset 4
    What is an Entrepreneur 6
    Mindset 9
Chapter 1 13
Your Child's Entrepreneurial Mindset 13
    Starting Early with Entrepreneurial Education 16
Chapter 2 24
Components of Entrepreneurial learning 24
Chapter 3 32
The Entrepreneurial Education 32
    Ezra and His Vending Machines 38
Chapter 4 42

The Challenges and How You Can Face Them..................................42
    Developing Entrepreneurship Skills In Small Children...............44
    Keeping your child excited about this mindset..........................46
    Teaching the Importance of Giving..47
Chapter 5 52
Understanding Active and Passive Income 52
    Is Passive Income better than Active Income? 54
    Why is passive income important? It's about your time............56
Conclusion 59

Description

It is widely believed that empowering young people with an entrepreneurial mindset is the key to developing more entrepreneurial behaviour and preparing youth to flourish in our emerging economy. However, little data exists to show a curriculum and education that leads to a more entrepreneurial mindset.

This eBook has been designed with a particular purpose in mind: the implementation of entrepreneurial measures in the home in order to help promote an entrepreneurial mindset in your child. However this book isn't just to get a child to be an entrepreneur, it's to teach so many other lessons that go along side this, the lesson of resilience, gratitude, and giving. This is a mindset that will serve any child for their entire life.

The true driving force for entrepreneurial behaviour is the mindset that a student develop towards the world around them and the lessons taught to them every day. This eBook demonstrates why and how to encourage the entrepreneurial mindset that will serve your child for years to come.

I hope to set a foundation in the research development of entrepreneurial learning model for childhood. I hope my eBook will show you how learning entrepreneurship can be done earlier in a child's life than most people believe.

I am so grateful you decided to purchase my eBook. I am so excited you have decided to take this on, and I hope you will have many ideas to take away and implement.

Introduction: The Entrepreneur and Mindset

As parents, it is our duty to train our kids well. Even if your parents didn't train you, it is your job to ensure that your kids grow with the right mindset. It was 2 years ago; I looked around my son's room and saw all the cheap broken toys he had. It was at that moment I wanted to figure out a way to ensure my son could begin to understand not only what went into buying those toys for him, but to also teach him the important concept of assets versus liabilities.

I watch other kids spend their money, actually their parent's money on overpriced shoes, clothing, toys and video games. Many of these kids if asked how these items were purchased wouldn't know or understand what it took to acquire the money for them. Many parents I found didn't talk about money with their kids or whenever the topic did arise it was just to say "we can't afford that." Don't be afraid to talk about money with your kids. They can understand more than you think. It's amazing how a phase like "we can't afford that" can make a child feel unsafe. Better words might be "This isn't a priority right now."

I believe the easiest way to bring the topic of money into your child life and have a wonderful effect on them, is to show your child how to fill their bedroom with assets and not liabilities. Show them different items in their home and answer the questions with them "what does this mean to you?" "Does it bring you joy?" What does it do for you?" Show your child how to assign value to material goods and how value is traded.

What is an Entrepreneur

Let's define what we are after. Entrepreneurship will simply refer to an individual's ability to turn ideas into action, specifically adding value and overcoming adversity to generate revenue. It includes creativity, innovation and risk taking, as well as the ability to plan and manage projects in order to achieve objectives. This idea supports everyone in day-to-day life at home and in society, makes employees more aware of the context of their work and better able to seize opportunities. Anyone can be an Entrepreneur.

The overall goal of entrepreneurship education is to give a child the attitudes, knowledge and skills to act in a entrepreneurial way, for either a commercial or non-commercial objective.

Why is it that there is no universal agreement whether entrepreneurs are born or made? First, entrepreneurs are born because there are some people who have come up with new business ideas that are currently recognized as successful businesses but these people were never educated on how to become entrepreneurs. On the other hand, entrepreneurs are made because there are some successful entrepreneurs who have studied entrepreneurship courses (diploma and degree programs) offered by mentors and school programs alike.

The Importance of Entrepreneurs.

Empirical studies show that entrepreneurship education positively influences entrepreneurial intentions on adults. Moreover, research shows that early formal entrepreneurship education increases children's propensity for choosing entrepreneurship as a career when they become adults.

The U.S. has been striving to keep its place in the world economy while facing problems such as financial and political worry, slow growth rates, aging population, and de-globalisation. In this context, the entrepreneurial activity is an important engine for economic growth and job creation. Entrepreneurship not only creates new companies and jobs, but also opens new markets and fosters development of new skills and capabilities.

According to one study, to get maximum growth and even better paqying jobs, each country needs more support for entrepreneurs. As such, different countries have been committed to promoting entrepreneurship education in its member states in the European Union. Many studies and writtings back this political decision since it suggests that, by developing entrepreneurial competences, as well as a positive perception about the need and the viability of the entrepreneurial activity. Simply put entrepreneurial education contributes to a increase of the number of entrepreneurs, and the number of entrepreneurs or those that can think think entrepreneurs contributes to the growth of economies.

Your Child's entrepreneurial mind

Children are actually born with an entrepreneurial mind, but it can soon become stagnet. Tomorrow's business leaders and startup founders are today's young kids whose parents have raised them with an entrepreneurial spirit -- a skill that is increasingly important as young people flood the startup world and the freelance economy.

As a parent, you inspire entrepreneurship by fostering the emotional skills your child will need, such as comfort with risk, effective problem solving, and a <u>positive attitude toward failure</u>.

"It's all about shaping the child's behavior," says Dr Andrea Vazzana, clinical assistant professor of child psychiatry at New York University Langone's Child Study Center. "Social emotional skills are important and the earlier you can help a child with them, the better."

Mindset

One thing most people will agree on today, is that it all start in the mind and in our thoughts. Entrepreneurial mindset is a combination of core beliefs and approaches to business which can breed success at an enormous level.

Whether you believe you're poor or you believe you're rich you are right. It is simply mindset, it is all about what we choose to think about. Being an entrepreneur is a state of mind. It is about analyzing the world and what is happening in terms of opportunities and possibilities, trying to understand how an individual intervention can enter the economic and social system in terms of construction and progress and then putting into practice objectives and translating ideas into action.

The entrepreneurial mindset is made up of some complicated ideas and beliefs however its strength and value cannot be undersold. To begin with, you should know that the entrepreneurial mindset is a belief that, above all else, a strong sense of what exact value you bring. Those who possess the mindset believe that life and business should be scrutinized at every level when any action is taken. A company's initial concept, its design, its sales strategy, you name it. All of it must be thought out with the utmost care.

How does an Entrepreneur use their mind

Great entrepreneurs possess the ability to view situations from an unusual perspective. They can see greatness in areas that the rest of us may view as average or even too difficult. This sort of sixth sense grants them the ability to see beyond a product or services potential.

Sensing opportunity and grabbing it before the moment passes are two vastly different things. Many people can see opportunity, but few act. However members of the elite entrepreneurial mindset tend to act on such opportunities before their effectiveness expires. They understand the importance of seizing the day which is one of the leading traits that helps make them so successful.

In terms of intelligence, those with the entrepreneurial mindset don't tend be be any smarter than average people. They just view issues and problems in a different way than the average person. They also seem to be looking forward to the future, which can give them a resilience many miss out on. This is why goal setting plays a big part (more to come). They are seemingly the polar opposites of reactionaries, managing to plan everything out before taking action.

Finally, never underestimate the importance of one's own mental and physical health, when you feel good about yourself, you make better decisions. While everyone understands that we live in a chaotic and fast-paced world, members of the entrepreneurial mindset must remind themselves to slow down on occasion being gratefull for the people and things around them. Running ragged is not the proper to manage a life. With so many important decisions to make on a daily basis your physical and mental abilities should be functioning at the highest level possible.

<u>So, can sensing oportunity, taking action, resilience, and mental health be taught at an early age?</u>

Chapter 1
Your Child's Entrepreneurial Mindset

Entrepreneurship is for everyone.

A recent study led by an independent research group, the Institute for the Future (IFTF) has predicted that 85% of jobs that will exist in 2030 have not been invented yet.

Disruptive technologies are radically changing the way we work and many of today's jobs will be transformed over the next decade. Businesses will become leaner and more agile, depending more and more on freelancers who come together for short-term projects. Workers will have a variety of different positions throughout their careers, many of which they have not been trained for. Even if you child will not run their own business they will need the entrepreneurial mind to know and have the confidence that they can figure any situation out.

It is nearly impossible to accurately identify the specific job-related skills that will be most needed in the coming decades; however, we do know something about the general skills, mindset and behaviors related to entrepreneurship.

The economic arguments for increased entrepreneurial education arise from the need for advanced skill development. Employers are increasingly demanding that people have the ability to recognize and take advantage of new opportunities. The World Economic Forum suggests complex problem solving, critical thinking and creativity will be the top skills needed in 2020. As traditional jobs become harder to find, these entrepreneurial skills are emerging as standard for creating economic opportunities.

Looking further ahead, the IFTF study concluded that in 2030 entrepreneurial traits such as vision, perseverance, creative problem-solving and learning agility will be critical for all workers to employ. To keep pace with emerging technologies and evolving skill sets, people will need to be flexible and adaptable, and be committed to continuous growth and development. Whether they work for themselves or others, they will need an 'entrepreneurial mindset', which can also be defined as "a growth-oriented perspective through which individuals promote flexibility, creativity, continuous innovation, and renewal."

It can be argued that an entrepreneurial mindset also leads to greater psychological wellbeing. The term is closely linked to the concept of growth mindset, a increasingly influential concept in education.

Students with a fixed mindset think they're 'dumb' or 'smart' in certain areas (like math, music or sports) and there is no way to change this. Students with a growth mindset believe they can build their skills with work and effort. Dweck's research has shown that students' beliefs about their intelligence play an important role in achievement at school and engagement in their lifelong education.

Students with a higher growth mindset are happier and achieve more. It then follows that an entrepreneurial mindset can also lead to happier and more productive people.

Starting Early with Entrepreneurial Education

A considerable amount of time can be required to educate your children to tap into their natural imaginations, to be more flexible, take risks, and to rise out of adversity.

Teaching and supporting this mindset and other behaviours from an early age should logically lead to higher levels of an entrepreneurial mindset, which would help push post-secondary level student outcomes to an even higher level.

Elementary school is where many people develop their intentions about their future careers, this is where you may hear you child say they want to be a police officer or a nurse. They are starting to see themselves in different career fields of life and looking to assign it to their identity. While future behaviours can be hard to observe due to time lag or the unpredictability of circumstances, research on intention models has shown that entrepreneurial intentions can be a powerful predictor of future behaviors.

Like strengthening a muscle, developing an entrepreneurial mindset and building related skills is an iterative process, requiring time, practice and repetition. In his comprehensive overview of entrepreneurship in education, Martin Lackéus recommends a progression model that builds from year to year, with entrepreneurship embedded into the curriculum as early as preschool and primary school.

The idea is that the continuum of learning helps students hone their entrepreneurial competencies over time.

Does Early Entrepreneurial Education Increase Entrepreneurial Mindset?

Many people question whether entrepreneurial skills and mindset can be taught effectively in the early years, or even at all. Some question whether "business" oriented topics such as entrepreneurship should even be taught in classrooms. As a concept, entrepreneurship is itself evolving. Rather than being viewed as a purely business-oriented role focused on maximizing profit with little respect for people or planet, entrepreneurship has also been increasingly seen as an approach to finding solutions to key issues and a distinctive way of looking at the world through the eyes of opportunity.

Early EMI Results: Exploring Changes in Entrepreneurial Mindset

The final section of the paper explores how students' entrepreneurial mindset changed during their participation in the NFTE course.* This analysis showed little difference between average pre and post scores, both overall and for each individual construct. But the averages masked a fair amount of variation in students' EMI scores: We found that roughly half of the students in the study experienced EMI growth, while the other half experienced a decline in their entrepreneurial mindset.

This variation allowed us to examine how changes in the EMI relate to growth in other, relevant entrepreneurial attitudes and behaviors. For this analysis, we relied on measures of entrepreneurial self-efficacy, entrepreneurship as an applied skill, and entrepreneurial intentions. We found that, compared to students who experienced a decline in entrepreneurial mindset, those whose entrepreneurial mindset improved:

- Are twice as likely to have growth in their entrepreneurial self-efficacy (i.e., 2.0 odds ratio);
- Are twice as likely to think about entrepreneurship as a skill that can be applied in any career (i.e., 2.0 odds ratio); and
- Have a 70 percent greater chance of wanting to own a business at the end of the course (i.e., 1.7 odds ratio).

We also wanted to understand whether the EMI was related to entrepreneurial knowledge. We found:

- The greatest gains in mindset happened in classrooms with the highest growth in entrepreneurial learning, while the lowest mindset growth occurred in the lower-performing classrooms.

Taken together, these findings indicate that EMI scores are meaningful and related to other areas associated with entrepreneurial thinking and behavior. This information is important for establishing the value and utility of the EMI. It also provides suggestive evidence that growing entrepreneurial mindset may have a positive effect in getting youth to see entrepreneurship and self-employment as a possible career path and something that can be learned and developed.

Similarly, the results suggest that helping youth develop the entrepreneurial mindset may in fact increase their intentions to start a business.

Here are the five parenting tips to help you foster entrepreneurial mindset in your kids. These will be discussed further in the following chapters.

1. Model effective problem solving. To prepare kids to find business ideas in everyday life, bolster their problem solving skills while they're young. When problems come up in your child's life, brainstorm solutions together. Help them identify the problem, think of all the possible solutions, weigh the pros and cons, and choose the best option.

2. Help them learn from failure. As a parent, you influence your child's willingness to try, fail, learn, and try again -- an essential skill for entrepreneurs. To do this, frame criticism as a learning opportunity by helping your child practice the skill or brainstorm what they could do next time differently.

When you offer suggestions for improvement, bookend them with specific praise on either side. "This is called a feedback sandwich," Vazanna says. "The child doesn't feel so harshly criticized; they can take away a positive message."

3. Let them make decisions. An entrepreneur's confident decisions are rooted in early independence. When kids are toddlers; you might give them the choice of spinach or broccoli with dinner or let them choose their outfits. "You're exposing them to what it feels like to make a decision, and helping them feel good for being able to do that," Vazanna says.

When kids are young, limit choices to a few options. "Kids can get overwhelmed if they have too many choices," Vazanna says. As they get older, loosen the reins and trust them with bigger decisions. Helecopter parenting is everywhere. This is where the parent is always around the child to often times catch the child just as or before they fall. But its in the falling that we all learned to walk. As hard as it is to see your child fail it may need to have so you can help them see the lesson.

4. Foster a sense of mastery. Entrepreneurs take huge risks, but being comfortable with uncertainty doesn't happen overnight. Kids needs the freedom to test their boundaries and master fears while they're young.

When your child faces a risky situation, help at first, then transition them toward independence.

5. Teach constructive ways to challenge the status quo. Kids are often taught to follow the rules without being explained why, a habit that inhibits entrepreneurship look at the modern classroom. It is set up for the teachers control — instead, teach kids to challenge norms constructively by articulating their rationale. Ask, what do you think needs to change, and why? What do you propose instead?

Great entrepreneurs are not born out of a desire to make money or to be famous. They can't imagine doing anything else. Building something new or improving on an old idea is the only thing that can make them happy. As parents, it's up to us to be realistic about the challenges of entrepreneurship, allow our children to follow their passions and adequately prepare them for living up to their full potential.

Chapter 2
Components of Entrepreneurial learning

Based on the findings in this dissertation, and by combining literature on educational psychology and entrepreneurship, this chapter theorizes on components to and dynamic processes of entrepreneurial learning. The chapter develops three propositions and a dynamic model that specifies how entrepreneurial learning can be understood as a process during which learners simultaneously and actively regulate their cognitions, emotions and motivations to reach goals, and that this in turn leads to development of entrepreneurial mindsets.

The Components of entrepreneurial learning

Research highlights a number of components of self-regulated learning, many of which are highly correlated. Although SRL has been studied from a range of theoretical perspectives, the role of goal-setting for self-regulated learning to occur has been highlighted across all disciplines.

This suggests that the components of entrepreneurial learning, defined as the simultaneous and active regulation of cognitions, emotions, and motivations to achieve goals, are

(1) cognitive awareness,

(2) affective awareness,

(3) motivational awareness, and

(4) the ability to set personal goals while understanding their relationships to the context in which they are set.

The cognitive component

The cognitive component is central for entrepreneurial learning to occur. Individual behaviors are determined by the interaction among personal, behavioral, and environmental factors.

Cognition describes how individuals process information, and cognitive awareness refers to thinking about one's own thoughts, what one knows, and the current state. It is a higher-order process that organizes what individuals know and think about themselves, a task, and the environment in which they operate to achieve goals.

This is where it all beings. You, as the teacher, parent or guardian can affect this on the biggest level. This is simply done by keeping the learning environment healthy. This is exactly like the term used in the business world of "culture." If you can ensure the culture or learning evironment is condusive to helping your child's thinking then you can greatly increase their drive and willingness to learn.

This can be as simple as maintaining positive communication in your home, for instance...

1. Ensure the environment allows for questions to be asked and answers to be sought out. If you child asks you a complex question show them where they can find the answer and if possible learn with them.
2. Keep the evironment more on the side of learning than entertainment. There is always room for entertainment, but learning should be rewarded.
3. Watch the words spoken in your house. There was a fantastic study done in the book "The Hidden Messages in Water" by Masaru Emotto where he described placing rice in two different cups with water. To one cup he spoke insults to and the other he spoke lovingly to. The cup with hateful speech started to stink and turn black. The other cup stayed white and gave off a fresh baked bread smell. I have done this experiment many times and I love it. You must remember your kids are made up of water and the words you use send a vibration which can affect them in many ways.

The affective component

Affect enables entrepreneurial learning. The affective dimension of learning occurs when individuals become aware of emotions in relation to a task, such as feeling interest, disappointment, shame, or pride.

Affective experiences relate to cognitive awareness in terms of knowing, perceiving problem difficulties, or confidence. However, the two components also have important differences.

This is where a child can be encouraged or absolutly crushed. This component must be handled with care. The first communication you must have with your child as soon as possible is the conversation of success verses failure. I believe failure does not happen until you quite. But even in failure lies the importance of the lesson which must be drawn out each time. Because if your child only sees the failure and not the lesson then the crushing blow could convinse them to not try again.

We must remeber to teach the power of preception. This is important to not only better understand yourself, but to better interact with those around you. Teach them to preceve not failures, but lessons. Not to preceve something as hard or easy, but as simply an experience.

This will be some of the most exciting part of your child to watch grow. They will amaze you by the stuff they can learn and do simply by changing their thoughts or emotions about the situation.

The Motivational Component

Motivation emerged as most important in understanding entrepreneurial learning, central for self-regulated learning to occur and important to individual ability to control and enhance the effort. This relates to the finding that motivation sustains individual perceptions of the ability to perform a task or achieve goals.

Every child is so different and therefore motivated by different things. I love learning what motivates my kids, because not only is it different in each child, but it seems to change with time. One thing that has not changed is the excitement they feel when something they wanted to do is accomplished. I love hearing them shout "I did it!" The key to motivation is seeing accomplishment, and for accomlishment to be seen goals must be set.

Goal Setting: I wish this was taught further in schools. We are for the most part taught to identify goals and then break them down to eventually accomplish them. But so many of us don't do it, why? It has to do with vision. Kids are asked what they want to accomplish and when a half hearted answer is give the teach makes them set the plan with said answer. Without it being a true vision you have just assign homework with little to no value.

A very important part of teaching this is to watch for the half hearted answer. Better yet watch for the vision that makes their eyes light up. Allow them to think about it for a while, not as part of a project, but as a means to identify their why. A way to allow them to discover what they truly want to build themselves into. Take your time with this one and you won't regret it. There are many books out there about identifying your vision or "your big why" as some call it.

Chapter 3
The Entrepreneurial Education

Entrepreneurial education involves developing behaviours, skills, and attributes applied individually and/or collectively to help individuals and businesses to create, cope with, and enjoy change and innovation. It involves high levels of uncertainty and complexity to achieve personal fulfillment and business effectiveness. EE represents an efficient and cost effective way of increasing the number and quality of enterprising graduates entering the economy.

Entrepreneurship competence is the ability to identify and seize opportunities and to plan and manage creative processes that are of cultural, social or financial value.

It requires a knowledge of contexts and opportunities, approaches to planning and management, ethical principles and self-awareness.

It includes the skills of creativity (imagination, critical reflection, problem-solving), communication, mobilizing resources (people and things), and coping with uncertainty, ambiguity and risk.

A entrepreneurial mind-set also includes the attitudes of self-efficacy, motivation and perseverance, and valuing the ideas of others.

For entrepreneurship education to be effective in developing the competences of learners, the capacity of schools to create supportive and stimulating learning environments is as important as is the personal competences and motivation of educators.

Entrepreneurship education cannot take place in isolation from the world outside of the school. It may requires working in partnership with external organisations in order to facilitate learning in other ways.

How entrepreneurial education can be promoted in your student.

One of the greatest challenges of the education system is to establish the suitable mechanisms for innovation and entrepreneurship to be considered important in the education process in all levels of teaching; in addition to promoting teacher training in methodologies that allow the development of innovation in teaching and learning processes. The specific challenge of entrepreneurship education is to be able to turn ideas into action. Traditional methods, such as reading assignments, review of old literature, exams, among others, do not activate entrepreneurship. Here are some ways to teach the things your child will need. Notice how many of them relvovle simly on asking questions. You would be very surprised about the power questions have.

Opportunity Seeking: It is important to show your child the ability of being aware of everything going on around them; as well as teaching them how to remain optimistic about what's happening and how they can affect it. As you go through your day and your child notices something allow them to expand on it. Ask them what they would do about that situation. Ask them what made them notice that particular thing.

Value Identification: Everything has value. Teach your child to analize the value in the things they want. Ask them what value certain things hold to them. Ask them to think about why something has value to someone else.

Problem solving: Throughout your child's life there will be so many obstacles they will face. The hardest thing for you to do will be to allow you child to problem solve the situation by themselves. You will want to do it for them because, maybe you're faster or you like that they look up to you. However, it will be very important for you to, in many cases, watch them solve the problem and simply be there to add another perspective.

Communication: The more questions you ask and the more you allow your child to explain their ideas to you. This will accomplish a couple things. First, your child will feel confident they can explain themselves. So many children these days find it hard to express themselves. Second, they will get used to the idea of asking questions to gain perspective and important information.

Risk: Allow risk taking while you are around to offer help when needed. Children are born risk takers for good reason. They need this ability to learn how to walk, to be comfortable falling down to achieve a bigger goal of walking and running. You can set up the learning environment to allow safe risk taking.

Resiliance: By teaching your child the lessons in the failures as well as the importance of being thankful for what you have and giving to those in need; you will see that it will become easier and easier for your child to bounce back when obstacles are meet.

These traits are being recognized as important for success in all areas of life because it is a pathway that enables people to address real-world challenges, seek opportunities and find new ways to create value.

How I am teaching Entrepreneurship to my son.

Because so little research and class availability is done at younger ages, entrepreneurial education occurs mainly during adulthood although the identification and assessment of potential entrepreneurs should happen during secondary education, when students are deciding on their future careers.

Nonetheless, some scholars conclude that in order to instil and develop important personal entrepreneurial characteristics in children, these should be enrolled in entrepreneurship education programmes, as that early stimulus might inspire them to choose entrepreneurship as a career later in their lives.

Ezra and His Vending Machines

Ezra, with the help of his dad, started EzeeVending, a Simple vending machine business at the age of Seven. This all started to happen after I saw the mess of cheap plastic toys in his room. I discovered I was teaching my son consumerism instead of entrepreneurialism.

Ezra had been saving his money in a bank account and it had grown to about $250. I asked him if he would like to invest that money instead of buying more cheap toys. It took some convinsing and we didn't really know what we wanted to help him do either. There were however a couple things I knew this investment had to accomplish. I would encourage you to use these rules as well for the identification and education of true wealth being, owning your time.

1. I wanted it to teach him how to run and grow a business. This meant it couldn't be a seasonal thing.
2. It had to have an element of passive income. This meant a lemonaid stand was out.
3. It had to be something we could do together. This meant lawn mowing wouldn't work. I have enough trouble with my own lawn.

We then discover vending machines while watching YouTube. This got Ezra very excited and he decided he wanted to buy two gumball machines with his money.

At the end of October, 2018 two gum ball machines arrived and we spent the day putting them together. While we put them together we discussed ideas about were they would be placed. The next day I ran Ezra though something called scripting. This is simply practicing what you will say to sell your product. Ezra needed to learn what to say to get his machines into different locations. Ezra practiced the line "Hi, my name is Ezra, could I put my gumball machine in your business?" over and over again for a couple days.

Soon it was time. We went to the first busines to see if they would accept Ezras machine. This was a person I actually knew well and I had prepared him the day before. I told him my son was going to be coming in and asking to place a machine there. I told him to feel free to say yes or no and that my son needed the practice. He was so good with Ezra. He asked him questions and they went around the place to see where the machine would best fit.

After that first machine placement Ezra was over the moon. I couldn' t get him to stop talking. It was great to see his confidence grow with ever conversation afterwards. Soon Ezra's understanding of his business grew. As he would get money he would re-invest into another machine and watch his earning grow faster. He also started to notice what machines made more money and why.

Now Ezra owns five machines and averages almost $100 a month, which is great for an eight year old. But some of the best parts of this business is the time I get to spend with him and the lessons I can teach him. I love the fact that he is understanding the concept of leverage and passive income and learning that he can do it.

One of my favorite lesson is teaching him tithe. This is the simple concept of giving 10% of his earnings away to church or charity. I don't know of too many great things than watching your child excited about giving money he earned to people that need it.

Now a big lesson! What do you do with the money they start to make. This is something you and your child will have to think about. The wonderful lesson I decided to teach my son was how to take that money from his sells and buy another machine and see how after that machine was purchsed how much faster his money grows. How far you go in this lesson and how much they want is entirely up to you.

Chapter 4
The Challenges and How You Can Face Them

Better knowledge about the impact of entrepreneurship education is one of the things that the education system is constantly looking for. However, so far there are only a limited number of studies on the effects of entrepreneurship education. I believe this has to do with the fact that its not so much a skill to be taught, but a lifestyle to be lived. This should be supported in the classroom and at home. If not in the classroom, then especially at home.

Despite the lack of evidence on the effects of entrepreneurship education, the critical role of entrepreneurial mindset must not be disregarded. Equipping young people with the skills needed for the 21st century, entrepreneurship mindset is a means to increased flexability and confidence and it can be a gateway for a greater integration of the framework for the key competences of lifelong learning.

Meanwhile, an increasing number of Member States, from the European Union are implementing national strategies on entrepreneurship education, which creates a platform that provides a opportunity where the impact can be measured in a European context and at a policy-level instead of at a project-level. Currently, the Member States are contemplating how they can measure the impact of their policies. It is important to ensure that Member States are not producing their own individual national measures, but instead that they will join forces to find ways to measure the broad impact of entrepreneurship education.

To move entrepreneurship education from being an extra-curricular 'add-on' to an integral part of a childs life involves:

- changes in teaching methods: greater use of experimental learning and a new coach/moderator role for teachers which helps students to become more independent and to take the initiative in their education;

- Allowing children to take a more active role in what interests them and what they want to build themselves into.
- A learning environment that doesn't stop in the classroom, but follows them home.

Developing Entrepreneurship Skills In Small Children

A teacher or mentor's mission is to nurture and provide incentives for the development of their students, turning them into individuals who will meet the challenges of the 21st century through versatile intellectual competence, a passion for discovery, resilience, and confidence.

> ➢ Will be challenged to fulfil their academic, artistic, athletic, and interpersonal potential by being

committed to performing their personal best at all times.

➢ Will become lifelong learners through the acquisition of competencies and skills to ensure they are focused, resilient, ambitious, curious, creative, and courageous, with a willingness to adapt to new situations

➢ Will be internationally minded adults by being taught perspective, value; and are reflective and their actions, critical thinkers, and have a deep sense of awareness of other people.

I understand this is very ambitious since it involves youngsters in very different age levels (from 3 to 18 years old). To develop an entrepreneurial culture, it is fundamental to ensure an entrepreneurial spirit in children and teenagers, and that can only be achieved by adjusting the teaching, its aims and methodology. "Teaching and learning to develop the entrepreneurial spirit involves so many different things. That's the beauty, there is no one way.

Keeping your child excited about this mindset

If you want to keep your child energetic towards his or her entrepreneurial career, here are 6 ideas for young or aspiring entrepreneur to help get you started.

You can encourage entrepreneurship within your kids by teaching them that:

- Any idea is a valid business idea
- Failure is okay as long as you keep improving
- A profitable business requires continuous learning and tweaking
- Creativity is what counts
- Being innovative makes you stand out from your competitors

Some of your child's business ideas will lead to great success, while others provide little more than a tremendous learning experience. Some ventures will prove to be highly profitable, while others may only produce a few dollars, if any.

The key is to teach your children to be resilient and keep moving forward toward their dreams. If your child's business ideas succeed, continue to encourage them to seek greater levels of success. If the idea doesn't work show them it was still a valid idea that could lead to an even better one. Along the way, continue to promote self-sufficiency, resilience, and confidence within your kids.

Teaching the Importance of Giving

Teaching your child the importance of giving back to the community is part of raising well-rounded individual. This lesson of giving can be taught in many ways, but for children activity is often the best way to keep them engaged while providing a valuable lesson about helping others through good deeds. One of the ways I teach my son is by having him set aside a certain amount of money he made and allowing him to give it to whom ever he wants to. This allows him to not be attached to the money and gives him a sense of looking out for someone that may need his gift.

Teaching kids the importance of social awareness and giving back to the community is vital to ensure your child grows to be empathetic, compassionate and caring. Volunteering and actively working to help others offers the perfect ways to help instill this lesson while making a difference in your community and the world beyond it.

Finding appropriate ways for kids to help out beyond the scope of their homes requires a bit of creative thinking and plenty of encouragement, but is a investment that's well worth the rewards that it brings, and it fosters an attitude of gratitude. This atttitude will prbably be one of the things that will serve them the best no matter what they decide to do in the future.

Some challenges you and our child may face:

1. Independence and Responsibility

This will be so difficult only because you will want to do it for them, mainly because they will be slow and you may be able to do it faster. Remember through this whole experience that it is about your child growing and doing things that other will say are way out of his or hers age group. At our house our kids are encouraged to be as independent as possible and to be proud of their independence. They are encouraged to be responsible for simple tasks, like tiding up tables after each activity, and to take care of their personal hygiene, such as brushing their teeth after lunch. Each has chores around the house. I have noticed these days chores have become a thing of the past. Remember above all, fight the urge to do it for them.

2 Self-esteem, confidence, and resilience

To reinforce the sense of pride about their own personal achievements, uses a system of positive reinforcement. One of the best ones I know is to simple tell your child how proud you are of them and what great work they did. Remember to praise the work and not the end task. It was the work that lead to the end of the task. If you start to only praise the end task this could make your child more suseptable to being crushed by failure or finding ways to cut corners.

It can be difficult to remember to praise the hard work. But rememeber its about setting up a mind that will be able to be both resilient and grateful. Nothing builds this like being proud of the work you did.

3. Willingness to take risks, withstanding failure, and perseverance

This skill can be easily worked in Sports and Physical Education lessons, but also in board games that allow a sense of cost for gain like Risk™ or Monoply™. Create the learning environment where your kids can feel free to take risks. But mostly they learn to overcome the sometimes overwhelming sense of defeat. While playing their favorite sport, they learn that they can achieve better results with hard work and team work (leveraging other people strengths). They also learn that after losing a game, instead of giving up, it is important to prepare for the next. Fight the need to protect your child from feeling a sense of loss. Allow the loss to happen, then, when it happens show them that a loss is not permenant.

4. Personal Control

Discipline is fundamental, as it makes children feel safer and also makes them learn to control their impulses. I love the saying atibuted to Wagner Clemente Soto who said "The inferior man argues about his rights, while the superior man imposes duties on himslef. Make sure you indentify the rules and follow them closly. A good example is organization. The last thing you want is for your child to have to learn this out in the world.

5. Preception

This will be a struggle throughout learning. But it can be even heavier when trying to teach the entreprenural mindset. Your child will speak differently and learn to see things in a different way. The may find it harder to relate with friends. You will have to have a conversation with them about how many people won't want to talk about the things they talk about. But you will need to teach them that although they may not be understood when they talk it is just as important to ask question and listen to those around you. You can then learn to provide a great value to many around you. This is the end goal of the entreprenuer. To provide a great service or product of value to those that need it.

Chapter 5
Understanding Active and Passive Income

Active Income

Income in exchange for services performed by a person. This includes wages, tips, commissions and income from businesses and employment in which he or she is actively involved.

Majority of the people live on the Active Income. They are required to trade in their time for money. Many people work 8-5. And many others need to work odd hours to earn a fix income. Most Active Income earners barely have enough money for retirement and they have to work all their lives.

They are tied down by their work and deprived of time. They don't have financial freedom, and they don't have time freedom.

I love those sunny summer days when I look out and see kids running lemonaid stands. I love the fact that the parents are letting them do that and showing them the importance of hard work. We can also along side this show them that there is also a way to free your time. This can be argued is true wealth.

Passive Income

Income from business, rentals, royalties or other enterprise in which a person is not actively involved in. For example, Robert Kiyosaki, the best selling author of "Rich Dad, Poor Dad" earns a passive income through the royalty of his book. He spent time writing the book once. His publisher will publish the book and the book stores will sell his book afterward. He does not need to be actively involved in selling his book but still receive an income regularly.

A person who owns a franchise business also earns a passive income through the collection of franchise fees from his franchisee.

If you own a property and decided to rent it, you can earn a passive income too. Ezee Vending, my son's business, runs kinda like a rental property. He buys a machine and fills it with candy. While he goes to school and plays with his friends that machine is working to bring him an income that he collect at the end of every month.

With passive income, your money works for you, instead of you working for your money. A minority of people lives on the passive income; hence there are few wealthy people. Being wealthy is truly owning and enjoying your time.

Is Passive Income better than Active Income?

Knowing, the difference between active and passive income, is very important and it could be the foundation that your child needs to build a sustainable financial future that will be devoid of financial worries. Passive income is essential for anyone who wants to learn how to make money work for them.

Here are some fundamental differences between active income and passive income:

Speed of income: Active income happens faster which is why many choose it. It can be seen and directly corrilated to the actions taken. Passive income take time to build and the outcome from the action many not be seen for a while.

When money is made: This is the best part of earning money through passive means. You make money rain or shine and even when you're sleeping. This is the kind of income derived from investments that you have made which constantly generate returns for you from month to month, year in, year out. For active income, you need to work and put in efforts in order to make money.

Income Potential: For active income source, your earning potential is based on your profession and the time you put into it. Passive income, on the other hand, provides a great opportunity for you to increase your earning potential. With eachnew investment your potential grows.

Effort Required: To earn active income, you have to actively put in effort, knowledge, and skills into the occupation or business. For passive income on the other hand, after the initial effort that is required to set up or invest, you do not have to continuously put in time to receive income from the passive source. You can also leverage the talent around you.

Lower Tax Bracket: In the United States of America and in most countries around the world, the kind of income that is taxed at the highest level are earned income, which is basically income from your active work. Passive incomes are taxed at lower rates, which means it provides tax advantages to people that earn their incomes from dividends, or rental income.

Why is passive income important? It's about your time.

Have you ever wondered why you were never ahead in your financial life? Are you frustrated with your job? You went back to college to obtain advance degrees hoping you will get a promotion in your job. Once you got the promotion you wanted, you probably started working harder than ever, many more hours when compared to the job you have before your advance degree.

Yes, you got the raise. But you realized your current job is limited by the number of hours you have in a day. No matter who you are, everybody has twenty four hours to themselves every day. Yet, everybody knows they can't be working twenty four hours a day nonstop. In other words, your income is limited by the number of hours you put in. Because of this, you will never get ahead financially no matter how hard or long you work at your current job.

Have you ever thought of having financial freedom? Financial freedom is when your passive income exceeds your expenses so you can choose not to work yet still be able to live the lifestyle you desire.

So why is having passive income important? Simple, without passive income, you will never be free. When you are free, you will have much more free time for yourself and your loved ones. You could travel the world without worrying whether you could pay your bills or not.

We are programmed from young that we should work hard for money. However, have you ever thought of money working hard for us? In other words, we get the most out of money with the least effort from our labor. Having passive income is like owning a cash machine that literally splits out money every day, week or month to you without you being there physically to operate the cash machine. Imagine receiving your monthly checks while reading your favorite story book on a beach in the Caribbean.

So do you think having passive income is important? I really think so! Do you want to be a prisoner to your job or be free to do whatever you want whenever you desire? Make your choice.

Conclusion

Fill your child's room and young life with assets and not liabilities.

We talked about many things, from creating the learning environment to instilling gratitude, resilience, and confidence. Remember to start with the vision and create the motivation. From there you are the guide that can ensure they will have a fantastic future.

Imagine if you had been taught this at a young age. It is now our responsibility to ensure our children learn to be more than consumers. Once someone has a comprehensive understanding of the way money and investments work, they'll have the confidence to make bolder moves when they're older. Even Warren Buffett teaches children about the connection between financial literacy and starting a business. And he's admitted that kids today know more than he did growing up. Keep your eyes on the future, and when your child is older they will be so glad you did this for them!

If you ever want to chat about ideas for your child entrepreneur, feel free to look me up on LinkedIn or Facebook. I absolutely love talking about this subject and the different ways we can teach it.

I wish you the best when it comes to developing this mindset in your family. I know it has helped us out tremendously!